A Lil' To
The
LEFT
Nefarious J. Dorsey
KE
LE

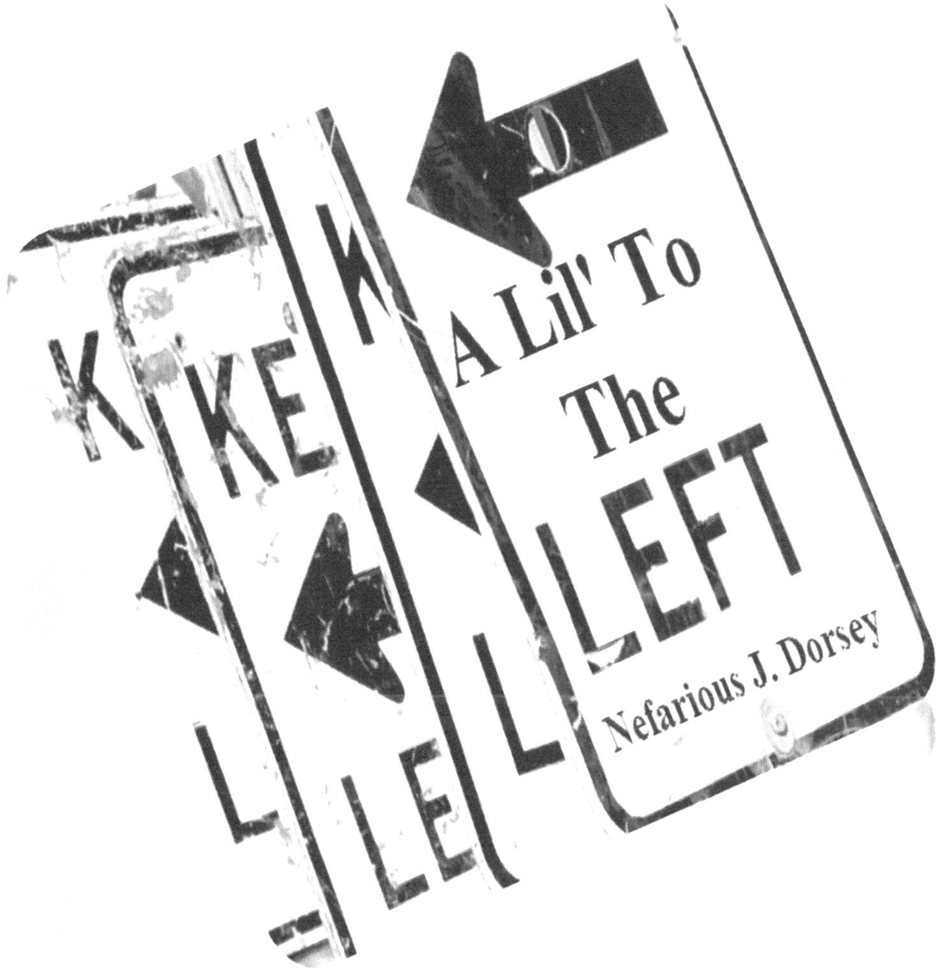

Copyright © 2020 Nefarious J. Dorsey

All rights reserved.

ISBN: 9798694552165

Table of Contents

Introduction

The left–right political spectrum is a system of classifying political positions, ideas and parties, social equality on the left to social hierarchy on the right. The intermediate stance is called centrism and a person with such a position is a moderate or centrist.

On this type of political landscape, leftwing and right wing are often presented as opposed, although a particular individual or group may take a left-wing stance on one matter and a right-wing stance on another; and some stances may overlap and be considered either left-wing or right-wing depending on the ideology. France is where the terms originated, the left has been called "the party of movement" and the right "the party of order"

A Lil To The Left is coming from the "left-wing" perspective and is entirely based on demanding social justice and equality for people who have been oppressed and victimized.

Acknowledgements

I want to thank God for the strength and the courage to put this book together. I want to thank my children Shanay, Mariah, Myriko and Gavin along with my grandson BJ and two granddaughters Zee and Tae'Shanay. I want to thank my mother the late Floried Dorsey-Tindall. I want to thank my sisters, Dr. Leslie Dorsey, and Marcia Dorsey. I also want to thank my brothers Keith, Aaron, and Paul (deceased)

I want to thank my editor Cryss A. Jones and my mentors Kiti Fowkles and Dr. Tina Jordan. I want to thank Baltimore City College Class of 1985 and all of the alumni from the greatest high school in the world. I want to thank all of those I didn't mention by name your continuous support and prayers are both needed and appreciated.

Somewhere A Bell Has Rung

Somewhere a bell has rung
As two men stand in the middle
Of the ring giving everything
They got
Taking shots at will
Displaying their talents
And skills for dollar bills
As the sanctioning body
Decides who loses
By the bruises and the brutality
Or the humanity and the
Sympathy of the referee

Somewhere a bell has rung
A butterfly flutters, a bee has
Stung another victim
As dark skin becomes the sin
Again as black men are hung
Swinging from the trees of
Hatred like pendulums

Somewhere a bell has rung
Because
The choir sung Hymn #9
As they caress the spines
Of those worn and torn
Choir books that adorn
The back of the pews
Where some feel the need
To read and follow along
Not knowing what is right
Or wrong

Somewhere a bell has rung
A flag is hung at half staff
Reminders of the lives
That have passed
As the task of mourning
Haunts our past
Anchoring our sorrows
To a path
Cause in the aftermath
We forget to laugh
Instead we try not to cry
As we remember those

Who die
Why?
Cause
Somewhere A Bell Has Rung
Reminders of the things
We have done
And worst
Just
What we have become

A Little To The Right (Old Mindset)

Standing here in my
Bullet proof vest
I am going to put
The second amendment
To the test as look up
The address and expose
This mess but this ain't
No Marilyn Monroe
You need to know
It's deeper than that
In fact the attack
On blacks makes
It Open Season
They need no reason
Cause the color of
My skin is the sin
So let me begin
If your hair is long
You must be doing
Wrong
Profiling me based
On a stereotype
Ain't right
So I write
In effort to ignite
Cause tonight
We are going to
Fight
No time for peace
So we are going
To take a piece
Cause peace is
Weak so to speak
The only thing
That's heard
Is not words
So hear my Mossberg
You want to
Engage my rage
Come test me
My testes are

Large
Come see who
Is really in charge
You now learning
Why Ferguson
Is burning today
We got an Uncle Tom
In the DOJ
I say that it is
Not a good day
In LA
I found injustice
In Chi-town
But the weather
Is no better in
Miami
B'more or
D.C
New York
And Philly
Only
Realize that the
Disenfranchised
Are everywhere
Do you dare
Engage our rage?
I am about to
Rip the page
Out of history
Cause his-story
Is forever tainted
Painted with
The brush stroke
Of lies
But he won't be
Able to deny
Or alter this truth
Cause the youth
Believe confrontation
And bullets are
The only way to
Change the situation
It is something that
We should expect

Cause there is a disconnect
From the sixties as
Shifts in political ideologies
Require fire cause the desire
For change will cause pain
But these chains won't be
Pulled or yanked
You can take that too
The bank
The ship has sank
The sharks are in
The tank
Get out the harpoon
Cause soon
We are going to
Turn the tables
Cause we are able too
I thought you knew
My political views
At first
Leaned a little to the right
I am always ready for
A good fight
I am going to exercise
My 2nd amendment
Right tonight
Is that alright?

Diatribe

My diatribe is hard
To describe
Because it has many tribes
But one chief
So my beliefs stretch
Far and wide
Although my Knee
Is Wounded
I am led to talk
About the bloodshed
As we have been led
To the slaughter
As they de-vaginalize
Our wives and daughters
Killing life from the womb
And soon they will join
Their husbands as they
Continue to disband us
No one understands us
Therefore we are unsure as
Our cries they continue
To ignore
Our pride swollen
As we are left holding
An empty bag
That we continue to drag
As we are shopping
For democracy
But still there are no
Groceries
For people like me
So my diatribe is hard
To describe as I inscribe
My insignia on their
Membranes
So they can ascertain
My pain
Over and over again
My thoughts become
Their thoughts
So they can see what
Is in my heart
And how their actions
Are tearing us apart
They mock us when they

Call us Engines or sqaw
But we only saw
Trains cut through the
Plains
Destroying reservations
As annihilation

Capsized

Because the truth
Has been watered down
We are left to drown
In the sea of inhumanity
Perhaps human dignity
Will dispatch out the Navy
To save us
As God is the only one
To have mercy on us
Because we can't
Get any compassion
From the leaders of
This land
So as a Black Man
I understand first hand
That the situation
We are facing
Although legally
We should
Not drown
Yet,
I haven't found
Anyone to rescue me
Individually or collectively
A I have found
That my race has
Been swimming
And drowning
Since the Trans-Atlantic
Slave trade was made
As the oceans
Of bigotry continue to wave
As the tides continue to
Allow equality to capsize
As we have come to realize
That we are alone
As they condone
Police brutality against
Minorities
As life boats continue
To float aimlessly
On the sea as all hope
Of being saved fades
With each passing day
Causing us to panic

As tolerance is our
Titanic
As we are
Trying to change
What they have done
Patience has become
Our Poseidon
As we will not
Be fictionized
Hoping humanity
Has realized
That we are not
Characters in a book
So step up and take
A look
Be brave and know
That we can only
Be saved from
A watery grave
If the captain decides
To override a direct
Command
Because that is
What compassion demands
No one should drown
In the sea of inhumanity
That includes me?
Perhaps they will
Dispatch out the
Coast Guard
Navy or
Merchant Marines
Out to sea
Still,
Patiently we float
Hoping that all
Is not lost
As some say
That the cost
For my people
Is too high and
That it is just better
To let Black folks
Die
As tug boats are
Still needed
To pull and tug
At humanity

Safely rescuing
Black citizenry and
Placing them on
The shores
Hoping to restore
Decency and
Rescue humanity
From this insanity
Hoping that when
The ship docks
That the hatred would
Stop
As the outcries of those
That survive
Will resonate
As true equality comes alive
Drowning hate
As navigate from
The Trans-Atlantic to
To the Titanic
Either way I have found
That we still drown
Only realizing that
Hope is capsizing
We have to be brave
As the waves of injustice
Are tossing us to and fro
One thing we know
We can't let go
Of our civil liberties
As we have earned
The right to be free and
Access to equality

Dear Whoever

Dear Whoever
I am hoping that
This letter would
Make me feel better
As I have some things
To get off my chest
So I can finally allow
These burdens of
Mine to rest
Right now life for
Us is a mess
As the civil unrest
Continues
To manifest
As we
March and protest the
Police brutality
Against minorities
Chanting that Black Lives
Matter
As injustice is served
To us on a platter
Cold at best
Served from the long
Handle spoon of lies
As our lives don't matter
As we won't survive
As equality should be
For the greater good
But we get far less
Than we should
Still no reparations
From this nation
Still we are facing
Annihilation
Still asking to be free
Since 1863
Another Civil War is brewing
As non-whites keep on spewing
Out their rhetoric and hate
But they better hope for
God's sake
That we don't hesitate
To retaliate against
Their hate

Because true absolution
Can only come from
REVOLUTION!!!!!!

<u>Down To The Water</u>

So I went down
To the water to be
Baptized only to realize
That there is no
Equality for me in the sea
And that the babbling brook
Took a look and
Started pretending
And changing
The message
It should have
Been sending
Instead of amending
It
I would
Have started transcending
Instead of
Causing me to descend
Rather than ascend because
Even in water there is inequality
Stretching from rivers to seas
To babbling brooks and racist
Streams
From tributaries and estuaries
The results rarely vary for me
Still the straits of hate refuse
To evaluate why the tides
Carry so much anger inside
And yet to their surprise
I still rise
Certainly and concurrently
Knowing one day I will be
Free
Having my ashes thrown
Upon the waters that
Refused to baptize me

19 (New Terrorist)

19 years ago to date
We experienced a different
Kind of hate
An act of terror
That simply couldn't be
Erased
As it became clear
That we had to face
Our worst fears
As coordinated attacks
In D.C. and NY
Left thousands to die
As the two towers
Fell from the sky
Leaving us questioning
Not the who per se
But the why
A slap on the face
Of democracy
As our own hypocrisy
Came back to bite us
As we really had to
Put our trust in God
As it was just an empty slogan
That we were holding onto
As it was stamped on
Our currency
But currently it showed
That we were liars
As the two towers caught
Fire
First responders were
Inspired to risk their lives
Trying to help those who
Survived the ordeal
As the appeal for vengeance
Had to be suppressed
Nevertheless
We had to start again
From Ground Zero
With new heroes and she-roes
With the same mission
But now with something different
As the paradigm shifted
Renewed hope was lifted

As many rejoiced and were thrilled
That Bin Laden was killed
But 19 years later a new
Terror emerged
That couldn't be purged
As the attacks on Blacks
Burned the nation again
Left democracy torn
And shattered
Chants that Black Lives Matter
Burn the night sky
As many Black Lives die
Under a new terrorist
As many pump their fist
To this
As the towers of decency
And humanity have come
Crashing down
Again we have to start from
Ground Zero
With different heroes and she-roes
That have regrets from
Yesterday and today
As we have lost our way
Again
When will the attacks on
Humanity end?
We can't forget then as
We remember what
Is happening now!
19 years later
The twin towers of decency
And equality
Have again come
Crashing down
To the ground
This time the terrorist
Are homegrown and
Are well known
As their actions are being
Condoned
Blacks are dying everyday
By their hands
As these attacks
Keep happening
All across the land
Yet, we must always
Remember

And never ever
Forget!

<u>We Are Here</u>

We are here
Not sure what that means
In relationship to
Where we are
Nevertheless we wait
With bated breath
Forced to inhale and exhale
Forced to accept the fallacy
Of this reality
That we've indeed have failed
We had no choice to accept
This because our voice
Has been silenced
Beckoning for violence
Because our history
Shows that's the only
Thing we do well
As hell maybe biblically
Based but the taste can't
Be erased as we face
This
Whatever this
Is it can't be dismissed
Quickly cause eventually
Always comes
When it is all said and done
As the desired outcome
Is rarely what we want
As we flaunt the lies
Until we die
As we dance with maggots
And flies
Still in death we cling
To the very thing that
Brings me back here
And will never disappear
The truth
So I begin again and say
We are here
Not sure what that means
In relationship to
Where we are Paradoxes don't stop
As they become the
New normal
That boggles the mind

While breaking the spine
Of Webster as these new
Words fester leaving
Tongues forked
As we are spoon fed
More lies
We wear the mask literally
Now and not poetically
Cause ethically and morally
Our folkways and mores
Fade with each passing day
Because when we kneel to pray
They prey on those that want
Change but pull and tug on
The chains of equality
Again and again
Kapernicking me but in the
End George Floyd-ing me
With a knee
So we are gregarious
As Corona is daring us
As I Nefarious stays
True to form as my cuneiform
Is scribbled and chiseled
A new way but delivered
The same by my own voice
As the vehicle to deliver
To the people
So the paradox doesn't stop as
Social distancing and having
Contact less contact
Puts me back to where I am now
Where ever that is
I am here
Not sure what that means
In relationship to
Where we are now
Nevertheless I wait

Different Priorities

She said that she was tired of
Marching and protesting
She was tired of the sit-ins
She was tired of the ambers
Going cold on fiery speeches
She was fed up that nothing
Was reaching them and him
She and they or me, myself, and I
She was now unsure
What we, what she and I
Were now fighting for
She said war changed me
She said that she wanted back
The person I was and not who
I am now
She wanted back the person I was
Before Uncle Sam
Manipulated my mind
Only to return home alone
Blinded by the doctrine
That alienated our kind
She says that I am now blind
That I refuse to be weighed down
By the reality of my skin tone
The fallacy has her now
Walking the picket line alone
A new war that is still
Cold and old for her
Leaving nothing for
Her to hold
Only memories of what
Used to be
A time to be free
Fist pumps in the air
Fighting for equality
Democracy
Fighting against
Hatred and bigotry
But that's not you anymore
Is it?
That is when she knew
But the warning signs
Were harder to ignore
Like you are doing now
Head hung low with your hands

In your pockets
As you now choose to do
Nothing to stop it
So now she inhales and exhales
Hoping that this Molotov cocktail
Wouldn't fail
And so she does what she does best
Upheaval and civil unrest
So she starts looting and shooting
In my soul
Hoping bullet holes
Along with grenades
Would blow up the mistakes
That have been made and
Put an end to this masquerade
No longer being suffocated
By the silence
As the violence and despair
Takes us there
Where the need to
Breathe and bleed
Would bring the soldier that
She so desperately needs
So her pain could be freed
As we could plant new seeds
So when they germinate
They could grow out of
Love and not hate
Giving you and me
The opportunity
To love all over again
Unconditionally
Until we both die
Not as enemies but
As allies

Forgive Me

Intercourse was forced
So it was inevitable
That we would divorce
Even though somewhere
Somehow we broke
Our vows
You couldn't forgive me
For my love affair
With her; life
I loved her more than
You, my wife
It wasn't by design
But there were numerous
Times
That she gave me something
That you failed to give me
Like love and honesty
She cradled my insecurities
She beckoned for my humanity
To rise up and take charge
Take action!
Her satisfaction and gratification
Depended solely on the situation
At hand
As I know that this is hard for
You to understand but
My skin color made me
Both a victim and a martyr
Both made things harder
On both us
As I put more trust in her
Than you
But you knew that already
As our separation was
Slow and steady
But I loved her for different reasons
As we have come to the end
Of our season
We know that things either
Die or grow
As reaping what you sow
Is biblical as these scars
Are visible
Still I am invisible to this
World

But life saw pass my faults
And gave me the things
That I needed in order for
Me to succeed
Although we all bleed
Fate gave us no choice
As the intercourse was forced
My voice couldn't be silenced
As these thoughts of violence
Changed me and although
It pains me
Having an affair with life
Feels so right although
To you it is so wrong
It would be hypocritical of me
To say be strong and that
It is for the best but
I must confess
She demands so much
And takes very little from me
I hope you will understand
That loving life was not
Part of the plan
But believe me when I say
I had no choice
She gave me my voice
And my purpose
I have only scratched
The surface
As my potential with her
Hasn't been reached yet
Although part of me has
Some regrets
I am hoping one day you'll

Forgive me for what I have done
And be happy knowing what
I shall and will become

<u>Principal</u>

To me it was very simple
To stand on a principal
And just relish in being right
So here I stand beating my chest
With all my might
As I yelled, I saw no one
Was in sight
So I won the war but still
Lost the fight?
Sometimes being right
Is so overrated
As I am frustrated
Thinking about what
I have done
As the desired outcomes
Leave me numb
Still I hum the sad song
That says I wasn't wrong?
Really, I know that sounds silly
But here I stand alone, again
On principal
Is it that simple?
Is it that important to
Be right?
Is it that important to
Win every fight?
Not sure that being
Right in every war
Is worth the price
And the sacrifice

New Leaf

Today I am going to say
That I am turning over
A new leaf
I am going to retire
The fire that I used
To uplift and inspire
Humanity
I will no longer use my muse
To shape the political views
Of a nation that is facing
Annihilation as the situation
Has finally taken its toll
On me
As the snores of the bored
And uninformed
Has finally worn me out
As it is so hard to be
Righteous
Political and
Socially Conscious
Trying to wake people
Up
As the nonsense has
Eroded away
Common sense
As the pretense
Never got so intense
Because people still sit
On the fence
Ignorant and indifferent
As making them aware
Gets you no where
People don't care
So now I am looking for
Some relief
Not going to be vocal
Any more about my beliefs
So I am turning over
A new life as I
Will write about rivers
And trees
Not mentioning
About lynching
No underpinnings
Or innuendos
All that political
Stuff I am throwing
Out the window
No more questioning

The status quo
Or telling people what I know
I am just going to go
With the flow
Just being a peaceful Negro
Forgetting about racism and Jim Crow

Great White Oak

Oh
Great White Oak
Why do you still
Lend them your arms?
So that they can continue
To cause me harm?

Oh
Great White Oak
I hope you know
That this ain't no joke
So,
Why are you choking
The life out of me?
Can't you plainly see
That my only crime
Is being a minority?
Still you are harming me
Under your cloak
You still dagger me
As I hang from the tree
Of Inhumanity and Inequality
There is no secrecy
Because what they have
Done to me
Has been done out
In the open
For all the world to see
So there is
No common decency
As their inhumanity
Has me
Swinging from
The arms of this
Great White Oak
Dangling from a rope
Until I choke and die
That is why
I say
That it is okay
Because
One day
You will pay
With your life
Violating the

Civil Rights
Of those who look
Like me
Who now are free
From the chains
Of slavery
Still I see
That you have
No remorse for what
You have done
You are guilty
By association
Your participation helped
To turn us from peaches
Into pendulums
You have been found
Guilty
For killing minorities
So
By the authority
Vested in me
You are hear by
Sentenced to death
By gentrification
You can't appeal
Your conviction
As the bulldozers
Will bring closure
To this situation
This is the hope
That no one else
Will choke and swing
From the ropes
Hanging from this
Great White Oak
The place where
My ancestors were
Hung from
No more human pendulums

In a world of rainbows
They
Devour us
They
Destroy us
and
Devalue us
Using and abusing our
Brilliant hues
At will
All because we let 'em
Knowing that
They only appreciate
The colors of hate
Black and White
With a few days of gray that gradually fades
Away
Slowly but surely
Like me

My Radicalness

I am coming from
The lower level
Where I just met the
Devil
Where he learned
That I was for real
When he got burned
By my truth
He could not refute
Because I am radical
Doesn't mean I am racist
Cause the basis of
My doctrine is not
Based on skin
Rather equality for
All of humanity
As the scales of
Justice fail to deliver
The promises of
The Constitution
So the only solution
Is revolution
As prostitution
Continues
So what's on the
Menu
Cause what is being served
Is deserved
Cause the price of black
Souls was cheap
Now the sheep
Are being led to
The slaughter
Now what's your order?
Jury nullification
Will give us gratification?
Can't get no support
From the courts
Understand we
Have to take
Matters into our
Own hands
Still newspapers
Assassinate me

Says I am radical
So I am the enemy
But in me
I just speak out
Against inequality
See the fallacies is
In their philosophies
Cause that's what they got
When they saw that
X marks the spot
Malcolm Little
Would tear into
A bag of skittles
But would not
Taste the rainbow
Cause these so
Called New Negroes
Think they have
Made it
Cause they have
Traded material gains
For some bundles of
Grain and a rimmed
Out Cadillac
They don't see the
Scratches on their back
They won't know how
To react
When the foot is
Deep up in their ass
They don't realize
That they are sinking fast
Cause they thought
In their heart
They would get a
Pass
Assimilation never last
Can't you hear them laughing
At your black ass

Dogma

Feet tired from walking
My dogma through the
Diatribe
As peyote induce states
Reverberate
Against the grains of sands
Under that I pontificate
Alone in a pulpit
Preaching to sinners and
Hypocrites
As I spit and spat
Facts perhaps traps
For the mind
As I spew knowledge
Out to empty pews
Who knew that when
They withdrew from me
That I would be free
To pursue thee
As my rhetoric
Runs like a river
Cause when I stand
And deliver
The eulogy for a fool
They shiver and quake
Not sure what to keep
Or what to take

Issues With Buses

Back in 64 we had to use
The back doors of the bus
And ride in the back because
We were black in fact it was harder
To ignore when a woman refused
To give up her seat and was arrested
Cause her feet were sore
So this defiance was hard to ignore
So this began the fight for Civil Rights as the issues remain
Nothing has changed
40 years later
They still hate us
This time to only find they are
Now
Throwing us under the same
bus
So now it is not about riding
Or them hiding their true intentions
Did I mention now their attention
Is now throwing us under same the bus
As the sound of the Greyhound
Crushes us
So who do we trust in 2020
It's not funny
It's clear that they still
Don't want us hear
So it appears that racism
Never disappeared
Now our hands are still up
Still stuck cause they
Don't give a fuck
That we still can't breathe
As
The wheels on the bus
go round and round
All through the town
We can feel the wheels
Of injustice
Go round and round
All through town and
On top of us
Every day Trailway drivers
Fail to display common courtesy
And decency to minorities
Some let me back track a little

In fact our issues with buses
Began in 1964 therefore
It's still hard to ignore
So now it is not about seating
Per se but the sound of the Greyhound
Makes when it hit the brakes

The Human Zoo

Welcome the Zoo, again
Who knew that part two
May and may not be for you
We got porch monkeys
Jungle bunnies
Soon to arrive 'coons and
Possum will be added to
Along with jiggaboos
At the human zoo

Shucking and jiving
A petting section
That is thriving
Cause that is what
They do so well
Can't you see that
Minstrel acts
Sell so well
Because of the
Tomfoolery and the
Buffoonery stemming
Back from the days
Of Slavery
African gorillas, chimps
And apes
Oh my
So they figure
That Niggas
Make exquisite
Exhibits
Just like Ota B
The Pygmy
Ishi was displayed too
In the human zoo

People pay to them
On display
Squirrels, jack rabbits
Sambos in Timbos
Pants sagging
Knee-grows

On display
In the concrete jungle
On display for free
In jail cells
Some caged up for
An eternity
Many
Have no idea
What it is to be free
As injustice sells wells
Many are sold for
Pennies on the dollar
Still they holler and shout
Cause they have a ring
Around their collar
It is hard to get the
Stains of injustice out
Cause the stains of inhumanity
Remain unchanged
As their chains rattle
Across the floors of
Injustice
While faith is the substance
Of things hoped for,
The evidence of things not seen
However, still today they
Are still on display
As jive turkeys aren't cage free
But will be free range
Eventually
However, that depends on
The Ringmaster's humanity

<u>Remember My Story</u>

I got on my traveling
Shoes
Because
I am about to pay my
Dues and get on the
Picket line and speak
My mind about these
Crimes that are happening
From city to city
No pity that's what got
Michael Scott shot
So I am leaving from
the valley in Cali
About to deliver some
Of that hate from state
But wait I am learning
That Ferguson is still burning
While authorities fear me
In OKC cause that racist
Chant was caught on video
But wait I am about to even
Up the score as I head to B'more
Another black man is dead
I am not going to be quiet
We need to riot cause it is
Nothing new cause the
Boys in blue think they
Are untouchable
But they are not
Cause what I got
Is some armor piercing
Ammunition
If I aim I am not missing
Cause I am on a mission

Tired of the senseless
Killing and bitchin
Now I am back in the
Kitchen
So sound the alarm
I am about to drop bombs
Come test me
I wish you try to arrest
Me
I am going down in a
Blaze of glory
Remember my story

<u>31</u>

When they say All Lives Matter
It is obvious they aren't looking
At mine
Because in this lifetime I have
Been victimized 31 times
Convicted of no crimes
As this is part of the design
That weighs heavily on my mind
Terms like BOLO or DWB
Are some of the excuses they
Use to profile me
Cause all they see is that my
SUV is not cheap by a long shot
So it takes at least 5 cops
To make a traffic stop with
Guns drawn
So how am I to move on
And let bygones bygones
When I wonder will this be
The day my family morns
Because I was born with
This deep dark suntan
So, make me understand
Your point of view
Because if you knew
What I have been through
And continue to go through
Then in your mind
You would understand me
When I say 31 times
Guns pointed at my head
31 times I should have been dead
31 times spread-eagled
31 times
Things are never equal
31 times I was almost
Like George Floyd
At least
31 times I have been
And continue to be paranoid

Stand Your Ground

I have found
That Stand Your Ground
Is nothing more than murder
Justified homicide
That collides and intersects
With my intellect
And the reason why Trayvon is gone
Stand your ground adheres to people's fears
As it appears to be lawful
It's awful
It's a tool that they use and abuse
Over and over again
When will it end?
Can I get an Amen?
They lied cause
The homicide
Wasn't justified
Time after time
They get away with
The crime
Just the other day
A man was blown away
He got shot over a parking spot
He died as his son cried
The murder was justified
Cause they found that
He stood his ground
So where was the fear
The tapes they said made it clear
That this law must disappear
As this pot of hate still resonates
With Zimmerman
Getting away shooting
Trayvon
We can't move on
The pot is simmering
And is about to make a mess
So I confess
That I have found
That the Stand Your Ground law
Needs to be shut down

<u>Few Remember</u>

I reached up from my
Coffin to feel the dew
On the blades of grass
That surrounded my grave
I saw the frost
had chrysalides
My tombstone

Hiding my name
My shame
My beginning
My ending
in a cocoon
A butterfly or moth
No more
I look around
To see what newbies
Could be found
Resting with me
In the ground

A dishonorable
Discharged vet
Missed the parade
To Arlington
A half folded
Torn trinket
Reminders
Of his failure
And defeat
For a country
That he pretended
To love

Over the hill
Malcolm
Martin
Rosa
Sat still
As they gazed
Upon Trayvon
Malice Green
Blood screaming
From the ground
As justice made no

Sound
Never to apologize
For taking their lives

Closer to home
Several unmarked
Graves sit alone
Legal executions
Sat the tone
It was time for them
To pay for their crimes
So the victim's families
Could have peace of mind

Unjust laws never saw
Him breaking her jaw
Or bashing her head in
Cause in the end
They knew he would
Send her to an early grave
Never admitting a mistake
Was made

Now the newbies can rest in the ground
Cause I have made my rounds
Now it is time I go back to
My nocturnal slumber
As I close my eyes and wonder
Whose number is next
As few remember while many
Forget

The New Math for Social Justice

When you postulate the hate then
Cube the issues
What remains is injustice and pain
Can anything break these chains?
3 nooses times 1 tree
Equals Jena 6
Then next thing that
Comes to mind
Is the Emanuel 9 times 1 shooter
Is the Charleston Theory of Negativity
An explosive theorem with negative
Ions that refuse to let
Bygones be bygones
So ignite the dynamite
Hate lit the fuse
Of this non-incendiary device
They that used detonation to end life
The same way 4 little black girls
Were blown away by the
Triple K's in the 205
Some years later
Instead of a bomb
You get the same effect
From, 1 knee on the
Neck of 1 black man
That is called the Floyd Effect
Still they postulate the hate
As injustice squared
Is rarely fair
As the truth is absolute
It always comes out uneven
Every time the formula is
Applied
Someone has died
As the remainder is a
Constant reminder
That the formula
Won't change
3 nooses plus 1 tree
Equal Jena 6
1 Black kid plus a soda
And a bag of skittles
Means very little
This is of course
Is obtuse

When in use is
The right angle
For the Zimmerman
Theory of Inhumanity
See how the hatred flows
Taste the rainbow
There's no pot of gold
For Negroes
American terrorism
Added to my activism
Has reactivated and
Rejuvenated my faith
Cause at bare minimum
The issues cube my faith
Mean that all I need
Is mustard size faith
Because of that I
Don't fear them
As my social theorem
Intersects with and combines
With my intellect
Corrects the formula
As Binary Zero Substitution or
Alternate Mark Inversion needs
To be converted
As square blocks
As taken away
By looting and shooting
As the only things that remain
Is hopelessness and pain
Because an object at
Rest stays at rest
Unless a greater force is applied
That is how Mr. Floyd died
You can't refute the truth
That this is the result of
Natural selection
That changes direction
But needs correction
Because that apply it
Are obtuse and they will
See the right angle
Cause the attacks on Blacks
Means the figures
Must be reworked and
Recalibrated
Cause the old conversion
And methodologies are outdated

Safe Poem II

You can relax
Outside your soul
You can play with
Other poets safely
You can take trips
Back and forth in time
Talk about trees
Beauty but not
About their bark
Or the lynching
Hidden in their
Trunks
Without having to
Stop or yield
No cautions on
How you feel
No long poems
About social ills
Or short ones
That call you to
Action
Blank TVs refuse
To show you the
News because
You will be afraid
That your cooking
Shows would get
Interrupted
While Ferguson is
Burning
What you need is
Comfort from
Complacency
You need milk
That never spoils
Lies that are not
Bitter
And truths that
Are gentle to swallow
You need safety
From a poet like me

Someone
That doesn't cause you
Any ripples or waves
In your consciousness
Something you won't
EVER GET FROM ME!!!!
You need a Safe Poem

Go Back To Africa

So America what exactly
Is the Reaction you are after
When you tell me
To go back to Africa
 I am trying to understand
When it was colonial migration
 Into African Nations
That brought my ancestors
From the Motherland Into another land
Sold on auction blocks
Picking cotton and Other crops
Fighting in wars
For a country
That chooses Slavery over Equality
 Inhumanity over decency
As our own complacency
Gives you consent Which is meant
That we deserve the
Treatment we are getting
Are you forgetting
That we built this country
Without us there would
Be no democracy
Therefore you can't
Afford to ignore
 Our demands for equality
As our pain forces us to
 Entertain violence
Because yet again
You take our silence As consent Which is meant
That the current paradigm
Needs to shift Because we can longer
Afford this anymore
We have to be stronger
Than tired clichés
So when you say
Go back to Africa
What exactly does
That mean?
When we have the dominant
 Genes, colors, and traits
 So biologically
 Shouldn't we be the
 Ones to hate
 Because you can't

Procreate
Because you are
Recessive
 Is this the basis
 For hating my race
As your behavior is
Excessive because
We made you and
You are mad
Because there is nothing
You can do
Except spew
Hatred and bigotry
 Because part of me
And my ancestors
Are part of you
And there is nothing
For you to do
Except to accept it
Because rejecting it
Will not change what
Is true Because
Biologically
We made all of you!

Still Violated and Unappreciated

Still he is hated
Still violated and Unappreciated
As he has graduated
From wooded stairs
To concrete
From splinters in His ass
Trying to avoid
Getting hemorrhoids
From sitting on the stoop
Unable to defecate or poop
Because there is a well
Placed boot in his ass
He doesn't get a pass
Because he can't get past
The stereotypes
That have shaped
His life
Born the wrong complexion
If lighter his life might have
Taken a different direction
All together because
Opportunities would be better
Than choices
As voices would display
Empathy because the
Privilege of being white
Is rooted in being superior
As everyone and everything
Else is inferior
Still we are not nearer
To a solution
What we need is a
Revolution or retribution
Still he is hated
Still violated and Unappreciated
He has made it?
As he has graduated
From wooded stairs
To concrete
From splinters in
His ass

Trying to avoid
Getting hemorrhoids
From sitting on the stoop
Unable to defecate or poop
Because there is a well
Placed boot in his ass
He doesn't get a pass
Because they can't get past
His skin tone
Only to remain invisible
And alone

<u>Seagulls</u>

Why do they pull
The seagulls
From my mental skies
Why do they shoot down
My truth With their lies
That's why the alibis
They provide
Still cause me to
Bleed from the inside
Forces me to **retaliate**
And because I fell
I am looking for
Another shell to
Protect me
From my enemies
Who don't want
To see me free
So they keep on
Hunting me
As they continue
To pull the seagulls
From my mental skies
Hoping that I die
Hoping that I falter
And alter my plans
But they don't understand
That no matter what
Anyone may say
Or
Do to my body
My soul remains free
Nobody has the right
To tell me how to
Live my life

A Little More Left (New Mindset)

When I write
Sometimes the right
Margins may be justified
As both sides may have lied
But I've cried more
As I am left
Knocking at the door
Of equality
No one sitting at
The table looks
Like me
Still I am fighting to
Be free
So I am left out
In the cold
With nothing to hold
Except my ideals
They will never
Accept how I feel
So they push me
A little more left
Though the margins
Maybe justified
But more people
That have looked like
Me have died
If you look deeper
You will find
That the left
Are the only ones
That are right in the mind
As their actions they
Have justified
As they have
Systematically
Nullified our voices
Limiting our choices
Forcing us to the left
Though the right
Margins may be justified
Both sides may have lied
But I've cried more
As I am left
Knocking at the door

Rhetoric

More Faith In Bullets

Greeting my brothers and sisters. I want to thank you for taking the time out to listen to these words that I will say unto you. First I want to give honor to God and his son that came in flesh form to rescue mankind from himself. As Brother Malcolm has stated I am not here to talk about my religious beliefs for if we do then that river that divides us will only get larger and deeper. So I am asking you to leave your religion at home and let's focus our attention at the issues at hand.

America has a problem, a problem that transcend the 244 years of slavery where Blacks are foolishly celebrating Juneteenth. I am not sure why they are doing so when we are still not free, and we are being executed in living color.

This is one of the fallacy that cripples Blacks in thinking that we are free when we are not. Just because you did not see the chains around you or you do not hear them rattling doesn't mean that don't exist when in fact they do. It is a fallacy in thought to think that because we have had a Black President for 8 years that we have indeed made to the top of the mountain but sadly we are still in the valley below. Obama's rise is deeply rooted in stratification. What does that mean? Let me explain.

Racial and ethnic stratification refers systems of inequality in which some fixed groups membership, such as race, religion, or national origin is a major criterion for ranking social positions and their differential rewards. Race is socially defined on the basis of a presumed common genetic heritage resulting in distinguishing physical "The differentiation of a given population into hierarchically superimposed racial groups. Its basis and very essence consist in an unequal distribution of rights and privileges among the members of a society" (Zuberi & Bonilla-Silva, 2008, p. 15).

A racial hierarchy is a system of stratification that focuses on the belief that some racial groups are either superior or inferior to other racial groups. The groups perceived to have the most power and authority are at the top of the racial hierarchy, while the groups perceived to be inferior are at the bottom. Racial socialization is the primary vehicle of cultural transmission for African American families, steeped in a tradition of resistance to oppression and embedded in "conversations and actions that communicate to [our] children how to survive with dignity and pride in a racist world." (Stevenson, Davis, & Abdul-Kabir, 2001 p. 46). So allowing Barack Obama to be President of the United States was nothing but a ploy to quell the unrest that continues to plague Black American. It was designed to pacify and to make Blacks think that they have made it and that the playing field is level when it is not. In actuality, electing Barack Obama to highest office in America only allowed the division of equality to stretch even further. The moral fiber continues to unravel as the blanket of inequality is the only thing that is covering Black America today. Do you think that it is a coincidence that after Barak Obama served his 8 years that systemic racism has become more blatant and overt. They are literally killing Black Americans and still with video can not get any convictions for officer's killing unarmed Black Citizens. Why are Breonna Taylor's killers free out on paid administrative leave? George Floyd? Trayvon Martin? Aiyana Stanley Jones- 7 years old executed in her home by SWAT Team and a jury refused to convict the officer that killed her? What about Jacob Blake who is paralyzed from the waist down that was shot 7 times in front of his three sons? Where is the justice? There is none.

So what I am about to say will probably ruffle some feathers but in order to make an omelet you must crack some eggs. To a certain degree I believe that marching and protesting has it's place. It worked for Martin Luther King Jr., Nelson Mandela, and Gandhi just to name a few. I believe that it was the best weapon for the time that it was used in and for. Today, I am not confident that marching and protesting is the best solution for the times that we are currently living in. Forgive me for a second as I digress just a little. How many times have your parents told you something over and over again but it not until they slap or beat you that you finally get the message. Isn't that the case here? Our cries have fallen on deaf ears, so it is time that we slap the face of America. How do we do that? I am glad that you ask.

If we are to continue marching and protesting then we also need to have weapons full loaded by our side. Since we are citizens of the United States then we should exercise our right to bear arms. We should police our own communities and not leave that responsibility to white America. If you haven't notice Jim Crow and the KKK have traded in their white sheets for blue uniforms under the doctrine to kill and enslave. We need to meet force with force. I know that this ideology might scare some of you, but I firmly believe that an eye for an eye is justified and warranted. Yes, some people will argue that leaves everyone blind, but I say we are not seeing the real issue here which is extermination and extinction.

We have nothing to lose and everything to gain. By any means necessary we must take the fight to our oppressors and let them know we will not stand for the injustice any longer and that we are prepared to die for this, equality, and justice.

We understand that there are causalities in every war, and this is no different. We have been in this war since 1863 as the bodies keep piling up. We must engage the enemy with the same vigor and disdain that they have been and continue to show us. If looting gets their attention then burn everything to the ground. I believe that violence has its place especially in the midst of tyranny and systemic racism. I also believe that the ballot box is another way to balance things out but considering how things have turned out I am not sure about that as a formidable weapon.

We have seen the Russian Scandal, the Bush Scandal with the votes in Florida, so as you can see, I am not confident that this system is working as it was designed to. Still there are issues with the Electoral College Process that still has not been fixed. So we can still cast our votes and tote our weapons as we need to engage our oppressor sending out a message that we are no longer going to stand or tolerate racism in any form, anywhere without a fight without guns first and with guns as a last resort. What I am saying is be vigilant and be prepared to fight this until the better end, even if that means death.

So in closing I will say this, it was 430 years the Israelites were in bondage, it took 244 years for slavery to be abolished, 8 minutes and 46 seconds for

George Floyd to die and 7 bullets in the back for Jacob Blake and Michael Scott who also shot in the back. We don't have a lot of time and unfortunately change is a slow process. We must use all of the tools at our disposal in order to win this war. It may take a combination of both peaceful and non-peaceful efforts in order for a change to come. We don't have 430 years; we don't have 244 years and we don't have 8 minutes and 46 seconds to spare. What we have is here and now. Ballots and Bullets go hand and hand for the times we are living in. I will travel the non-violent way first and will use violence as a last resort. They have declared war on Black America it is time we do the same to the **white** moderates that are controlling America. I have more faith in **bullets than** I do the ballot box.

<u>On Being Naïve</u>

This is probably naïve for me to say but I thought racism only existed in the United States and at the time of such thought South Africa because of apartheid. I did here some isolated issues in Europe and Australia but that did deter or detract my thinking that racism was a problem exclusively in the United States of America. As technology grew I have learned that racism is a global problem that is as infectious and deadly as the Corona Virus. Unfortunately, the internet has brought out the worst in humanity and I have seen it at its worst. On Facebook, I have been asked to assist in moderating a large group of people that is about 90K members in it.

When you enter this group the title page says Poetry Is Everywhere: Black Lives Matter. Displayed are various clenched fist that are different hues of Black. So there is no surprise that when you enter this group what this is all about. In my short time as being a moderator I have seen the worst of humanity in full and living color. I have seen Black members being bullied and ostracized, criticized, and marginalized. I have seen the chant "All Lives Matter" as a means to thwart and minimalized the effects of this movement.

This chant is very racist as it displays the ongoing bigotry that continues to plague the world globally. It is not enough to agree to disagree, however, some of the members want to take it to the extremes which prompts moderators like myself to take actions because the racist behaviors violate the rules of the group. A group this large has shown me how deeply ingrained racism and prejudice has gotten all over the world.

I have seen racism in Ireland, London, New Zealand, and Australia. It appears that if your skin is dark that you cannot escape racism and bigotry anywhere. The open use of the word Nigga, monkeys, jiggaboo, sambo along with the chants "go back to Africa" have come across my screen more times than I can count. It makes you wonder what has an indigenous race of people have done to warrant such hatred from everyone? What is more interesting is that our culture is embraced as everyone wants to Black but not be Black.

Everyone profits off Black People and then turn around want to hate us on the other hand. Even as we speak, corporation are siding with BLM only because they know that if they don't it will impact their bottom line. It is the new slavery, or should I say corporate lynching because Blacks have the tendency to make others rich while staying poor. The infighting amongst Blacks only serves as another source of contention.

The internet has given rise to cyberbullying and a platform for people to spew their racist rhetoric. It also allows people to be cowards rather than face to face contact. In the group that I was asked to assist in moderating, in a span of 12 hours I had to remove, block, and delete some of the most racist posts that I have ever seen in my life. Need I remind you that I was born between two civil rights icons Martin and Malcom. I thought that Jim Crow only existed in the United States, however, sadly I am wrong. The internet has allowed me to see the worst side of humanity.

People all over the world just want a reason to hate and it appears that they are greater in numbers than those who want equality and justice for all. I am angry that the world got to see and hear the deaths of Trayvon Martin, George Floyd, Breonna Taylor, Jacob Black, Aiyanna Stanley-Jones and so many more dying at the hands of the New KKK and Jim Crow.

How disheartening is it to know that racism is global and is more infectious than Covid-19. Where did humanity go as it seems like it cannot be found anywhere. Love and kindness have been abated and abandoned.

Democracy is not highly favored as the most sort after form of government. Our failures in voting has allowed the stench to infiltrate the nostrils of humanity and the world.

With the current President we truly have become the clowns of the world. Technology has provided a vehicle for people to carry out hate speech and bigotry with no penalty. The sad part is that there is only so much you can do as people can create new fake profiles anytime they want. As a moderator I can block them all I want but they still can come back in with a different profile. This is a war that we can't win ever. For me to make that statement shows how bad that problem is. Sadly enough I do not think that will ever change as the world is devoid of humanity and good will to all. It is easier to hate than to love. Loving someone takes a special skill because you have to see the individual as a person rather than an object of disdain and hate.

Urgency of The Moment

I no longer have faith that this country will do right by Black Americans. I also believe that marching and protesting is a useless way for Blacks to achieve equality in this nation. Sometimes you have to take what you need from whomever is holding it and keeping it away from you. Justice and Equality have been the carrots that have been dangled freely in the faces of Black America.

No matter how hard or how long Blacks try to reach for equality it is always yanked away or only inches away from the grasp and reach of Black Americans. I believe that it is time for Blacks to adopt a Black Nationalist philosophy instead of the We Shall Overcome ideology that has been practiced throughout history with leaders like King, Gandhi, and Mandela. Their methods worked for the times that they had encountered. It makes no sense for me to turn the other cheek and expose the other side of my face to again be struck by your enemy. This type of ping pong action only offers pain and patience along with foolery.

I understand that at some point in time that the enemy gets tired and then eventually concedes to your demands, but the question is how long does that take to achieve? The one thing that we do not have is time. I have spoke on this time and time before, the Israelites were in bondage for 430 years and slavery was abolished in 244 years. Who has that kind of time to wait? I say no one does. George Floyd died in 8 minutes and 46 seconds.

The current leadership is fueling the fire by spewing out rhetoric out to the country and at the Republic National Convention give a speech that was 1 hour and 19 mins and spoke nothing about the current condition that the country is in because of his failed leadership. It appears to me that the current President could be reelected again if people do not get out and vote but again it is all up to the Electoral Colleges again.

We cannot survive another 4 years under the current administration. How many more people must die in order for the rest of America to see that we need change and we need it now not yesterday but today. Everyday someone Black is either shot or killed by the police and nothing is being done about it. The AG a Trump puppet has not done anything concerning the rise in police brutality against Blacks. Breonna Taylor's killers are stay free out on paid administrative leave and no charges have been brought against them. Aiyana Stanley-Jones 7 years old was executed in her home and the jury refused to kill the officer that killed her.

You have high profile athletes speaking out for equality and still nothing is being done. So what is left to do? Adopt a Black Nationalist ideology. The marching and protesting are not working so instead of offering our cheeks we need to arm ourselves and teach our children to do the same. We need to defend ourselves against the tyranny that exist.

I am sure that when they see Black Citizens exercising their 2nd amendment rights the paradigm will shift to the correct position. It will be at that time that they would want to talk about real change because the fear of Blacks arming themselves is something that would put fear in every white moderate's mind. Fear of a Black Planet was not only a hip hop classic but simply states the consistent fear that white America has in their minds. How many officers would think twice about police brutality if they knew that the community that they were policing all had guns and were permitted to have them legally? I promise you that police brutality would come to a screeching halt.

Suppose there were laws that stated that shooting an unarmed citizens would automatically be a conviction of 1st degree murder with a hate crime element added which could open the door for the death penalty; how many officers would think twice about shooting or harming unarmed citizens. Right now there is no accountability and because of that extreme measures have to be adopted in order to get the situation under control.

Any officer related shooting should place the officer or officers on unpaid administrative leave and if they are cleared of the charges then upon reinstatement would be eligible to get the back pay. If you simply take away the incentives to shoot someone than the likelihood in theory that police brutality would decrease.

Now I know there is a great risk in my thinking, but something has to be done. A Black Nationalist strategy could cause more bloodshed along with the threat of Civil War but aren't we at war right now in the streets? The only difference would be that we could meet force with force because right now we are at a disadvantage. My strategy is about leveling the playing field and once that is done than our oppressor will be ready to sit down and talk about real change because the paradigm would have shifted to our favor because we are armed.

In closing I will say that the time is now for us to get justice and equality here in America, however, they will not give to us freely so we must take it and when we do we must be armed. I know that this ideology will come with some bloodshed, but I say we already bleeding now so what if more blood has to be shed. It was colonial migration that brought our ancestors here to America in the hull of slave ships.

It is the idea of democracy where their words say liberty and justice for all and since they wrote in a document called the Constitution then it is our right to demand what that document says, each and every word uttered by the forefathers of this country and we will not stop until the spirit of that document is achieved. The urgency of the matter has again called for us to be treated equitably like the rest of the American citizens of this nation

Letter To These Divided States

The recent events have led me to a conclusion that I have overlooked for many years and now have realized; we should not expect anything from you, America. You have a history of treating people that you deem inferior differently when it was your ancestors that went into the Motherland and brought black bodies to work the plantations of this land. When you defected from British Rule you came to America and stole from the Indians after they taught you how to survive on the land.

The reward you gave them besides blankets laced with chicken pox was death, annihilation and near extinction. You have a history of lying, cheating, pilfering all in the name of and for this place you call the United States of America which has never been "united" and probably never will be. It is an unrealistic expectation to think that after over 400 years that you will allow the documents of freedom to apply to all of your citizens. I will say with great vigor and disdain that America will never allow the blanket of equality to comfort Black Citizens.

We have to accept that the fallacy of the American Dream has been a nightmare for anyone with dark hues. The signs of marching and protesting are merely toothpicks in which the majority pick their teeth with only to discard them on the floor of humanity and decency. I no longer expect for you to do right by us and it seems that the only thing left for us is violence. Violence and war are the only things that you are good at and seem to understand. I don't condone violence per se but I do not abhor its use in certain situations.

I am indifferent when officers are shot and or killed as my Hammurabi eyes may have me blind to the situation at hand. The Civil War was about slavery and though it may have ended in this history books, I still say that it is still waging on even up to this moment to include the grand jury in Louisville failing to convict the officers that killed Breonna Taylor. How ridiculous is it that you fail to convict the officers and yet want to pay out 12 million dollars in a wrongful death suit. Whether it is 30 pieces of silver or 12 million dollars, no amount of money can cover the debt that is owed for life and fair and equal justice. We are asking a country that had language in the13th amendment that Blacks were 3/5's of a person before it was ratified. So what am I saying here? I am tired of talking, let violence lead the way.

www.ingramcontent.com/pod-product-compliance
Lightning Source LLC
Chambersburg PA
CBHW051310160726
47994CB00003B/1393